T0149237

RAISING
GIRLS INTO
EXTRAORDINARY
YOUNG WOMEN

A Mother's Perspective

Monica Hawkins, Ph.D., M.P.H.

authorHOUSE®

AuthorHouse™
1663 Liberty Drive
Bloomington, IN 47403
www.authorhouse.com
Phone: 1 (800) 839-8640

Published by AuthorHouse 10/18/2018

ISBN: 978-1-5462-5640-3 (sc)
ISBN: 978-1-5462-5639-7 (e)

Scripture quotations marked KJV are from the Holy Bible, King James Version (Authorized Version). First published in 1611. Quoted from the KJV Classic Reference Bible, Copyright © 1983 by The Zondervan Corporation.

Scripture quotations marked NKJV are taken from the New King James Version. Copyright © 1982 by Thomas Nelson, Inc. Used by permission. All rights reserved.

This book is dedicated to our extraordinary son Therman Hawkins III, his future children, and his future grandchildren.

Table of Contents

INTRODUCTION IX

CHAPTER 1 A VISION FOR YOUR
EXTRAORDINARY
BABY GIRL 1

CHAPTER 2 BE READY FOR YOUR
DAUGHTER'S BIRTH 5

CHAPTER 3 THE BENEFITS OF
BREASTFEEDING
YOUR BABY GIRL 7

CHAPTER 4 CULTIVATE YOUR
DAUGHTERS INTO
ENTHUSIASTIC READERS... 13

CHAPTER 5 SHAPE YOUR
DAUGHTERS MINDSET 15

CHAPTER 6 DEVELOP ECONOMIC
REASONING IN YOUR
DAUGHTERS 19

CHAPTER 7   PATHWAYS TO BUILD
             SELF-CONFIDENCE IN
             YOUR DAUGHTERS 21
CHAPTER 8   INTRODUCE YOUR
             DAUGHTERS TO
             HEALTHY FOODS 25
CHAPTER 9   SPEND QUALITY TIME
             WITH YOUR DAUGHTERS ... 29
CHAPTER 10   FOSTER OPEN
             COMMUNICATION
             WITH YOUR DAUGHTERS ... 35
CHAPTER 11   FAMILY
             INTERACTION TIPS
             AND GUIDELINES 37
CHAPTER 12   KEEP YOUR
             DAUGHTERS SAFE 41
CHAPTER 13   CONTROL YOUR
             DAUGHTERS
             ELECTRONIC USE 45
CHAPTER 14   HELP YOUR
             DAUGHTERS ACHIEVE
             ACADEMIC EXCELLENCE 49
CHAPTER 15   ESTABLISH ATHLETIC
             GOALS WITH YOUR
             DAUGHTERS 57
CHAPTER 16   LOOK AHEAD IN
             YOUR DAUGHTER'S LIFE ... 65
NOTES 67

Introduction

This book will change you and your daughter's lives. It is written for every infant girl born so that she will grow up to be one of society's successful and extraordinary young women. It is a known fact that there will be many obstacles that you and your daughters will face throughout their lives. Unfortunately, society sometimes finds it hard to accept extraordinary girls as being successful, but my life's mission is that your daughters will become successful anyway. I want your daughters to always exude self-confidence, mental strength, intelligence, and other similar characteristics in every situation they encounter. I want these same characteristics to be developed in your daughters so that they can always stand out in a group setting. I want your daughters to always be noticeable in a group setting in positive ways. This means that they need to be self-confident in every situation they encounter so that individuals will always recognize them for being extraordinary. I know that this is easier said than done and that your daughters may get extremely nervous sometimes, and that is totally understandable. The more that your daughters practice being self-confident, they will soon begin to feel more comfortable each time displaying self-confidence. As an extraordinary parent, your job is to always create a safe place for your daughters to be raised. This environment should include giving them basic needs such as food, water, shelter, and tender love and care and much more. Spend time displaying love and affection toward your daughters. You owe it to them so that they can then display love and affection toward their own children when they become adults.

I want to pass along my blueprint to raise your daughters to be mentally-strong, articulate, intelligent, and extraordinary young women and leaders who should be taught each of these characteristics from the moment they are born. I am a true believer that you are what you think. So, if your daughters believe that they are extraordinary, then they will be extraordinary.

I want your daughters to always stand out from other young girls because of their leadership skills and great character. From the time that your daughters are young teach them to be self-confident and to be happy with who they are and to never change themselves just to fit in with other girls or society. Make sure that you have numerous discussions with your daughters to let them know that some individuals in our society will not always treat them with respect. Prepare them for a tough society where they may encounter negative individuals at some time during their lifetime, but teach them to remain positive to deal with these types of situations. It is very important that you teach your daughters to think positive thoughts about themselves and know that they can accomplish anything in life that they want. Teach them that once they set goals for themselves that nobody should ever get in the way of them reaching their goals. Parents, you can raise your daughters to be intelligent, self-confident, and extraordinary young women and leaders if you follow my blueprint. "Train up a child in the way he should go, and when he is old he will not depart from it (Proverbs 22:6)."

CHAPTER 1

A VISION FOR YOUR EXTRAORDINARY BABY GIRL

Parents, have a vision in mind for your daughters from the moment you know that you are having a baby girl. Envision that your daughters will be extremely intelligent and extraordinary and that you will always want the best for her. A support system for your baby girl at an early age is extremely important for her. When your daughter is an infant consider enrolling her in a day care center that is very close to your home. Consider taking an extended amount of time off from your job. This will allow you to spend as much time as possible with your daughters during the initial stages of her life. It is extremely important that whenever your daughters wake up that she constantly sees her mom's face filled with tender love and care. Staying at home with your daughter, when she is a baby, will be some of the best times of your life. You will see her first everything. Her first smile, roll over, coo, and sip from a sippy cup. While your daughter is a baby, spend a lot of quality time with her. Spend time walking around the neighborhood with her. This is good for both of you. It is good for you because it will give you an opportunity to shed those excess pounds that you gained during pregnancy. It is good for your daughter because she will see the beautiful world that surrounds her.

Expose your daughters to all types of soothing and relaxing music when she is inside your womb. Every night, before your daughters go to sleep, turn on classical and other relaxing music on the radio on her nightstand. Start this routine when she is a baby. The music will soothe her as a baby and as a toddler she will quickly grow to love listening to classical and other relaxing music.

Your closeness as your daughter gets older will first begin with your closeness when your daughter is a baby. It will help to contribute toward your daughter always being self-confident and extraordinary. Teach your daughters that her parents will always be there for her no matter what situations that she will face in her life. Another vision that you should have before you are pregnant with your daughter is that you are going to breastfeed her. Every mother should consider breastfeeding her daughter. A good reason to consider breastfeeding your daughter is because it will help her immune system to become strong. As a result, she will rarely get sick as a baby.

CHAPTER 2

BE READY FOR YOUR DAUGHTER'S BIRTH

Address any problems that will possibly affect you being a great parent raising your daughters into extraordinary young women and leaders. If prospective parents are stressed in their lives, then it may not be the best time to have a child. Consider waiting until you are not real stressed out. Having a child is the most unselfish thing that a woman can do. Once women have children they must always prioritize and put their child's needs and wants before their own. This sometimes means not buying or waiting a little longer to buy some of the items that you want to instantly buy. A lot of women forget this and put themselves first. Once a woman is pregnant with a child she must remember that life is no longer about her but about her child. Selfish parents will usually produce a selfish daughter. Train your daughters not to be selfish. If you do not train them to be unselfish then they will grow up to be users and takers instead of givers. Your daughters deserve the best life that their soon-to-be parents can give them. When a woman is pregnant she should consider reading to her unborn daughter. Your unborn daughter will constantly hear her mother's voice, which can relax and calm her while inside the womb. Also, sing to your daughters when you are pregnant. A mother's voice can be calming and can help build a natural and physiological bond with your daughters. It is imperative that your unborn daughters are surrounded by a warm and calming environment.

CHAPTER 3

THE BENEFITS OF BREASTFEEDING YOUR BABY GIRL

Breastfeeding is a process where a woman feeds her baby directly with milk from her breast or from a breast pump. Breastfeeding is the most naturally occurring thing that can happen during childbirth.[2] The size of a woman's breast does not have any impact on whether she will be able to successfully breastfeed her baby.[2] Before a baby is born, prolactin is produced by the pituitary gland.[2] Oxytocin, also produced by the pituitary gland, is a hormone that stimulates the breast to eject milk.[2] While a woman is breastfeeding her baby, antioxidants are released in her milk. These antigens help to keep a baby's immune system strong. Human milk contains all the healthy ingredients that a baby needs. Some of the healthy ingredients contained in breast milk include protein, sugar, fat,

7

and antibodies. Prolactin is a hormone that is widely known to relax a woman and make her feel happy and joyful. Oxytocin is widely known to cause strong feelings of love between a woman and her baby and is released during breastfeeding. Breastfeeding produces an emotional satisfaction between a mother and her baby. Babies that are not breastfed get sick more often than those that are breastfed. Babies that are not breastfed usually catch colds quicker and sometimes get more ear infections.[2] Breastfeeding a baby also decreases their risk of Sudden Infant Death Syndrome (SIDS).[1] Breastfeeding may seem intimidating, but women can talk to their doctors about their reservations. Find support groups that are available in your area to help you successfully breastfeed your daughters. Breastfeeding is an extremely pleasant experience if your husband/partner/friend is supportive of you breastfeeding your daughters. His decision to support you may heavily influence whether you breastfeed your daughters or not. Talk to him about the benefits of breastfeeding. According to the American Academy of Pediatrics and the World Health Organization, they recommend that a woman breastfeed her baby for a minimum of six months and to continue with breastfeeding for a year after solid foods are introduced to the baby.[2] There are psychological benefits to breastfeeding your baby.[2] The closeness that the mom and baby experience is priceless. There is a physical connection that you two will hopefully share for the rest of your lives.

Every mother should consult with their doctors before deciding whether to breastfeed their baby. There are some instances when a mother should not breastfeed their baby due to a medical condition.[2] Before a woman has a baby, it is an excellent idea to attend a breastfeeding class so that she learns as much as possible about the issue. Hospitals have lactation specialists, nurses, pediatricians, family doctors, and breastfeeding support groups to help a mother get started with breastfeeding her baby. It has been well-documented that breastfeeding may increase cognitive development in a child.[1] Hopefully, all soon-to-be moms will consider breastfeeding their babies. When a woman decides to breastfeed her baby, it takes planning ahead whenever she decides to go out with her baby.

A breastfeeding support system is available to all mothers for several months after they have a baby. The support system may include other women that are currently breastfeeding or used to breastfeed or the lactation specialist at the hospital. Every woman should consider the benefits of breastfeeding even if she was not a breastfed baby. Mothers should try to maintain a healthy diet while breastfeeding. An advantage to breastfeeding is healthy eating will always benefit your babies. Once a woman starts eating healthy to breastfeed her baby, her good eating habits may continue throughout her life. It is more acceptable now to breastfeed in public than it was in past years.[2] So, a woman should not feel embarrassed if other individuals are around while she wants to breastfeed her daughter. A breast milk pump is available for mothers to use when they are resting from their baby or they need to return to work. When a mother returns to work she may want to think about continuing to breastfeed her baby. A lot of employers have lactation rooms available for breastfeeding moms. This would allow a mother to breastfeed her baby even longer.

As soon as your daughter is born, the two of you will start sharing a very strong emotional and physical bond with each other. Hopefully your daughter is a baby that naturally takes to breastfeeding. You can tell that she enjoys it based on the relaxed and calm look on her face whenever she is breastfeeding. Words cannot describe what it will feel like. It will be breathtaking whenever you watch your daughter look up into your eyes from time to time while she is breastfeeding. You will feel such pride and joy from knowing that you took the time and effort to do this with her. You should also breastfeed your daughter because breastfeeding her will contribute toward increasing her cognitive development. You will absolutely love breastfeeding your daughter knowing that it is the best thing for her. Consider staying at home and breastfeeding your daughter for as long as you can. I know that every mom cannot afford to stay at home for a lengthy time, but if you can it is worth breastfeeding your baby girl and waiting until she is older before she starts going to a day care center. So, when your doctor asks you if you are planning on breastfeeding your daughter, it should be an instantaneous "yes."

CHAPTER 4

CULTIVATE YOUR DAUGHTERS INTO ENTHUSIASTIC READERS

Start reading books to your daughters when they are inside your womb. It will allow them to explore and wonder about their surroundings and will also expand their curiosity once they are born. Even if you do not enjoy reading books, your daughters will love that you took time to read to them. This is especially important when your daughters are preschool age so that they begin forming and learning new words. Reading is a way to boost your daughter's educational knowledge as they get older. In this society, your daughters are being raised in an environment where they need to answer more than just yes and no questions. They need to learn to answer questions that require them to have a conversation with their parents or other individuals that are talking to them.

Before your daughter can read, always read to her every day. Read a lot of books to her. When she is younger, your daily routine can be to bathe her, rub her body, and then read to her before she goes to bed. At night, whenever you finish reading to her you can turn off the bedroom light and leave her bedroom. Whenever she wakes up at night you can turn on the light in her bedroom and then read a book to her until she falls back asleep or sing to her. If that does not work, then you can turn on quiet classical or other relaxing music on her radio. As your daughter gets older and becomes an adolescent, make her take more time to read books. One way to do this is to limit her cell phone and social media use and to have her to take along a book in the car as you ride out for appointments or errands.

CHAPTER 5

SHAPE YOUR DAUGHTERS MINDSET

Why are so many girls satisfied with being average students? Oftentimes it depends on what the girls think about themselves. If your daughters think that they are smart, then they are smart. If your daughters want to be an Honor Roll student, then she must think that she is an Honor Roll student. Why is it that the same two students receive the same information in a classroom and one of the students does extremely well and the other student does not do well? It is the mindset of both students. One of the students thinks that they will do well and the other thinks that they will not do well. It is important that your daughters strive to do well all the time. Some of them will do well in school but striving to do well in life is just as important. Your daughters must keep telling themselves that they will do well at something and believing it so much that they do well. Your daughters need good role models around them so that they can emulate them. The role model does not always have to be their mother or father. The role model can be another family relative or somebody else like a teacher, coach, or close family friend that is involved in raising them.

It is always important for your daughters to think positive thoughts and know that they can do anything in life that they want. The more that your daughters think about themselves in a positive light the more that good things will happen to them. Have you ever known an individual that always speaks negatively about various issues? Whenever this individual does this then negative things usually happen to them. Whenever your daughters think positive, they will exude more self-confidence toward other individuals. Also, positive things will usually happen to them. If your daughters speak about negative things, then negative things will probably happen to them. I am such a strong believer about this. It does not mean that everything positive will happen in your daughter's lives. It means that the negative things will be hopefully kept to a minimum.

Raise your daughters to be mentally-strong young women. All things are possible with God who strengthens me (Philippians 4:13) is a Bible verse that your daughters can recite every day. Parents, discuss with your daughters "Positive Affirmations" and how important it is for them to speak positive words that they believe about themselves to themselves and out loud too. Help your daughters to come up with their own "Positive Affirmations" for themselves and post them somewhere in the house on a vision board where they can see and repeat them every day. It is very important that your daughters arm themselves with a self-confidence armor before they leave the house every day.

Your daughters should post their "Positive Affirmations" on vision boards that they can look at every day and train their minds to think positive thoughts each time. Hang a collage of pictures on the vision board highlighting every achievement that your daughters made each school year.

Your daughters will not achieve academic success in their lives overnight. One of the first educational lessons that you should teach your daughters is that whenever she works hard at her school work, that she will do well. It will take years of vigorous training and sacrifice that will pay off in her life as she grows into a young woman. Groom your daughters for countless hours to prepare them for academic success.

CHAPTER 6

DEVELOP ECONOMIC REASONING IN YOUR DAUGHTERS

Teach Your Daughters About Money

Constantly teach your daughters about the value of money. Arm your daughters with the necessary financial tools for them to be successful in life. It is imperative that you teach your daughters how to make money and budget their money for their financial life. It is important that your daughters become financially stable so that they can provide for themselves later in their lives. These skills are needed to build financial wealth and freedom and allow your daughters to live their dreams. Set up a college savings plan when they are young. Take your daughters with you to the bank to open an account in their name. Whenever you conduct transactions with their savings, checking, and money market accounts they should be at the bank with you as much as possible.

CHAPTER 7

PATHWAYS TO BUILD SELF-CONFIDENCE IN YOUR DAUGHTERS

It is very important that you know what your daughters think of themselves. It gives you a measuring stick to gauge whether you need to work more with them to build their self-confidence or whether they are on the right track to being self-confident. Self-confidence is built on your daughter's successes in life. Your daughters should learn from their failures too. Teach them not to be afraid to fail. So many individuals are afraid of failure and never risk learning or growing more because fear holds them back. Even when your daughters lose, they win because of all the lessons that they learn from losing because with failure people do not try. Failure should be a great motivator to your daughters to improve themselves. If your daughters try something once or twice and fail, then they should want to try again. When your daughters have a strategy that aligns with a purpose, things will happen. Things will happen even if your daughters do not want them to. Tell your daughters all the time to keep living their purpose in life with a strategy in mind. There will be moments when things will not go right and moments when everything goes right for them. So, as great parents teach your daughters this so that they can survive when things do not go their way.

Encourage Your Daughters To Be Self-Confident

As parents, you do not ever want your daughters to suppress or hide their feelings from you. Also, parents should not want their daughters to be afraid of their reactions whenever they do something wrong. Your daughters will gradually learn to have a balance between expressing certain feelings and controlling other feelings. This comes with maturity so, until then, be patient with them. Encourage your daughters to ask for what they want in life. If they do not, then they will never get whatever it is they want in life. Some current school systems are not instilling leadership characteristics into young girls. Therefore, it is so important at home to reinforce to your daughters that it is perfectly okay for your daughters to be great leaders at school and other places as well. It is disheartening to watch some of our young girls not being groomed to be extraordinary young women and leaders. Instead, a lot of them are being groomed to be followers and not great leaders. Too many girls are not being developed to their full potential because they have not been encouraged by their parents or the school systems to be self-confident. Teachers sometime email parents about the most minor issues. It almost seems as though they want the girls to behave perfectly. No young girl is always going to behave perfectly. It seems that there is no system in place that allows girls to make mistakes and not be perfect. As a result, some young girls are becoming less and less self-confident and assertive. They are not taught to fight back in certain situations or stick up for themselves. If they do fight back then they always get into trouble and are chastised for doing so. This can sometimes lead to them always feeling bad about the way that they handled a situation. This is not necessary. As a society, we need to learn how to better teach young girls that it is okay to make mistakes. At home, parents should take the time to instill in their daughters that it is okay to make mistakes.

Encourage Independent and Inquisitive Thinkers

Let your daughters know that it is okay to think outside the box. Parents, raise your daughters to be extraordinary thinkers and not ordinary thinkers. More extraordinary thinkers are needed that are creative and not afraid to take risks in business, science, or any other career field they choose to pursue. As great parents you should want to raise inquisitive daughters. Whoever your daughters associate with should be just as smart as your own daughters so that they can learn from them as well. Great minds think alike. Your daughters should be encouraged to always ask a lot of questions. Once she answers one of your questions, the answers should lead her to ask more questions. She should never take anything that you say at face value but always want to go into more depth to understand an issue more.

Do Not Force Your Daughters To Change

One of the best things that parents can do for their daughters is to try and let them naturally develop into their own beings. Gently guide them into their next stage of life so that they can become young women of good character. If your daughters are having difficulty adjusting to a different stage in their lives, try and be as patient as you can with them. Give them the room to make errors. It may take your daughters a little while to adjust to the change.

Chapter 8

Introduce Your Daughters To Healthy Foods

Do not allow your daughters to eat a lot of sweets or candy. They should eat plenty of vegetables and fruit. Allow your daughters to experience grocery shopping with you and try to make it fun for them. It is critical that your daughter's practice having healthy eating habits to prevent diseases such as obesity later in life. A stronger effort is needed from schools, teachers, counselors, and parents to monitor young girls eating habits and educate them about diseases such as obesity that may affect them now or in the future. Parents, talk with your daughter's teachers at schools and ask them to assign research projects on the long-term impact of obesity on heart disease, high blood pressure, and stroke and to discuss healthy eating habits with the students. Your daughters could research obesity and offer suggestions on how to better address this issue. Parents can informally monitor their daughter's eating habits at school and at home. Make sure that your daughters are drinking and eating healthy snacks like peanuts, almonds, dried fruits, juice, and sports drinks instead of eating a lot of candy and drinking a lot of sodas. Make sure that the menus that are offered at your daughter's schools provide more nutritious options for them such as salad bars and baked foods rather than French fries, hamburgers, pizza, and other fatty and greasy foods. The school systems should consult with dietitians and nutritionists on selecting healthy menus.

A Poster Session on Obesity can be a program that you suggest is held at your daughter's school. Awards could be given for the best poster that could be judged on content, presentation, and comprehensiveness for first, second, and third place. Public health professionals and various community members from the local areas could serve as judges. The participation by these individuals conveys a passionate sense of community support and interest in the students' education and well-being. An Obesity Awareness Day could be held each year at your daughter's school. Public health professionals could be invited to participate and lecture on issues related to obesity. Private representatives could also be invited to staff booths and informally talk with students about the issue. Brochures and pamphlets could be distributed to the students that discusses obesity. If your daughters are exposed to healthier foods in their school environment, then they may become more passionate about eating healthy and change their eating habits. The Poster Session on Obesity and an Obesity Awareness Day and other health issues could then be duplicated at the regional and state levels.

CHAPTER 9

SPEND QUALITY TIME WITH YOUR DAUGHTERS

Pick a special time each day to pray together as a family and worship together as well. Praying will show your daughters that they should never be too busy to spend quality time with God. This will help them to build their own relationship with God and reinforce Christian characteristics such as compassion, courage, self-control, love of others, faith, perseverance, godliness, and kindness. Your relationship with your daughters will also be stronger. Pray about various topics affecting your family.

Teach your daughter's life skills such as cooking so that they will learn to be independent and be able to take care of themselves. Your daughters should also be taught how to clean, wash clothes, and wash dishes. Always make time to talk, play board games, listen, and constantly interact with your daughters.

Your daughter's homework and class work should be reviewed on a regular schedule. Spend some extra time practicing school work with them so that they will do well. Praise your daughters for the school work that they have done well, and explanations should be given about why they got an answer wrong. Parents should be patient enough to explain concepts to your daughters again and again if they do not understand it the first time. Hopefully they will ask questions if they do not understand a topic.

Videotape your daughters whenever they participate in school activities, sports, church activities, and day care center activities. Download the videotapes to CDs or to the computer for their enjoyment as they get older. Keep a scrapbook for your daughters that allows them to see pictures of themselves, book reports, letters, special art projects that they made in school, camp, and other places. Write letters to your daughters on special holidays (Easter, Mother's Day, Hanukkah, Christmas, Kwanzaa, Thanksgiving) and other special occasions like birthdays and graduations throughout the year and describe their special accomplishments and goals that they have set and met for themselves. Consider laminating their letters and other special items such as sports certificates, honor roll certificates, and other important certificates and put them in a portfolio for them to cherish later in their life.

Always be encouraging and motivating to your daughters with positive words so that your daughters know how proud their parents are of them. Do not let your daughters ever take for granted that they know that you are proud of them. Try to limit the amount of time that you talk on your cell phone or home telephone, unless it is an emergency, while you are talking, playing at the park, or spending quality time with your daughters. Many parents seem to make the mistake of constantly talking on their cell phones while they are in grocery stores, at the mall, at the park, and other places which takes time away from your daughters. Tell your daughters as often as you can how you feel about them and how much you love them. It will help to build their self-confidence. Always send messages to your daughters that they are valuable to you and are always worth your time. Whenever you spend time with your daughters, be sure to keep your focus directly on them and not anywhere else. Spending quality time with your daughters is important. The more time that you spend with your daughters when they are young will establish the more time that they will want to spend with you as you get older.

It is extremely important to take quality time to talk with your daughters to answer questions that they have about their lives. Taking time to talk with them as they get older is even more important. Especially when your daughters begin adolescence. A parent can never turn the clock back in time and wish that they had spent more time with their daughters if they did not when they were growing up. So, the lesson learned is to not take time for granted and spend as much time with your daughters whenever you can. I know of a lot of women that put more time into their careers than their daughters. Some women can balance their careers and motherhood well, but others are not as successful at it. Unfortunately, some of these women that are not able to balance motherhood and their careers well may realize later in their daughters' lives that they should have spent more time with them when they were younger. Sometimes this is because these women did not have the necessary time to spend with their daughters because their jobs were so demanding. Also, these same women are a lot more stressed out from their busy jobs, which causes them to have less patience and love to show toward their daughters. This can lead to their daughters possibly becoming withdrawn from them and feeling depressed. If you notice any serious behavioral changes or signs of depression in your daughters, then make sure that you get the necessary help for them.

CHAPTER 10

FOSTER OPEN COMMUNICATION WITH YOUR DAUGHTERS

After picking up your daughters from school, ask them how their day was. What happened? What did they have fun doing for the day? What did they not enjoy doing for the day? Ask if there is anything they want to share with you. Always take time to listen to your daughters. Allow them to talk about any subject with you. When they know that you are truly listening to them it will validate their feelings. Hopefully they will then be open with you about comfortable as well as uncomfortable topics. You should always want your daughters to feel comfortable enough to talk with you about any subject. They will hopefully want to confide in you and not keep any secrets from you.

When your daughters turn around twelve or thirteen years old their doctor will normally ask you to step out of the room during physical examinations. I am sure that a lot of parents may be uncomfortable with stepping out of the room, but the doctors want your daughters to have an open dialogue with them because they want your daughters to trust them. They want your daughters to feel comfortable enough to ask them questions if they do not want to ask their parents about or discuss certain issues with them. Parents should also want their daughters to have open communication with their doctors in addition to themselves.

CHAPTER 11

FAMILY INTERACTION TIPS AND GUIDELINES

<u>Parents Should Be Teammates</u>

It is extremely important that parents work together to raise their daughters. One voice should be heard by your daughters to prevent unnecessary confusion among them. Your daughters need to see that both of you have a good relationship with each other by being loving and respectful toward each other. Oftentimes, your daughters will naturally emulate what they see from their parents and other adults that they trust. Parents should split household duties between themselves and then alternate checking homework with your daughters. Mothers, it is important that you leave your "power heels" at the front door when you get home after work every day and become Mommy to your daughters. It is okay to be a powerful career woman but be careful about wanting to control everything at home and not compromise with some issues.

Schedule "Me Time"

Parents should take time away from taking care of your daughters throughout the year. Everybody deserves to take a break from parenting. Being a good parent takes a lot of time and effort. A break will give parents time to recuperate and recharge your energy level. The break can be for a short or long time. Hire a babysitter or ask your family or friends to take care of your daughters while you spend time with yourselves, others, or doing something else that you enjoy. You will feel so refreshed when you do this, and it will allow you to be extremely patient with your daughters.

Discipline Your Daughters

Discipline is needed in all homes. Your daughters may not know the importance of being disciplined but your daughters need discipline in their lives. I have talked with a lot of teachers that tell me that the girls that come from homes that have more discipline are the girls that are better able to focus in school and accomplish goals they set for themselves. Discipline gives girls structure and organization that makes a difference about how they respond to things in their own lives. There are always opportunities for parents to use discipline as teaching moments for your daughters to set them on the right path in life. These moments will stick with your daughters throughout their lives.

Whenever you discipline your daughters, try to spend a lot of time explaining things to her. Then she will know why she is being disciplined. Do this as much as possible instead of yelling at her about everything. Explaining things to her will allow you to help her understand her thinking process instead of her focusing on how angry you are. Even though you may be extremely angry many times, it is more important for her to understand why you are angry and what she can do the next time when she is faced with the same kind of situation. It is imperative that you let your daughters know that everybody has made mistakes in their lives. It is not how many mistakes you make that is most important but that you learn from those mistakes. Nobody is perfect and no one in this world is immune from making mistakes. Tell your daughters that it is okay to make mistakes in life but that she must always learn from the situation and try not to make the same mistake again. Sometimes your daughters will make the same mistakes, but they should keep trying anyway.

Offer Incentives To Your Daughters

Reward your daughters with incentives when they do well in school, sports, and other activities. The incentives do not have to be expensive. They can be small tokens such as video games, gum, lollipops, money, clothes, books, or restaurant meals. Incentives such as these will give your daughters something to look forward to when they do well. Rewarding your daughters can also help them to feel a sense of accomplishment. This will also help build their self-confidence and self-esteem. Incentives will help them work hard at whatever they are trying to accomplish. Also, your daughters may challenge and push themselves to do even better the next time at something.

CHAPTER 12

KEEP YOUR DAUGHTERS SAFE

Always make sure that you know your daughter's whereabouts. They do not necessarily have to be right next to you, but you should at least know their whereabouts and what time they plan to return home. Parents, it does not take a long time to lose sight of your daughters, especially if your daughters have enough time when you turn your back and they can walk away. Since parents know that this can happen, it is imperative that they keep as close a watch on their daughters as possible. Do not let your daughters go to a public restroom by themselves until they are a certain age to be able to handle themselves in a dangerous situation. Once they start going to the bathroom by themselves, parents should still stand outside the bathroom door for safety reasons. Anything could happen to your daughters in the bathroom if an insane adult or older child has enough time to harm them. Be careful about leaving your daughters alone with an adult that you do not trust. Be careful with whom you let spend time around your daughters. Your daughters should usually be around other girls that are about the same age as them. For the most part your daughters should not be allowed around girls that are much older than them. This can be unsafe. There are some exceptions to this of course. Never ever put your daughters in a situation that could potentially lead to them being harmed or molested. Do not allow your daughters to go over any other girls' houses that you do not personally know. Going to the mall, playgrounds, and other places should be off limits with other girls whom you have never even met before. Invite your daughters' friends over to your house or set up play dates with them. This gives parents a chance to observe their daughter's social style. Parents will be able to intervene with discipline when needed, individually or as a group. Peer pressure will usually begin to become a major factor in your daughters' lives around seven or eight years old. So, your daughters must be self-confident and comfortable when interacting with other girls by this time, if not earlier.

Bullying and Self-Defense

Bullying has been occurring more and more to young girls as time goes by. More measures need to be put in place so that your daughters will not be afraid of other girls. Your daughters should be taught how to defend themselves. Unfortunately, in this day and time, at least once in their lives your daughters will probably be teased by another girl. Regardless of where you choose to raise your daughters this will happen. Girls can be very mean and cruel to each other. Some of the girls that are doing the bullying may be raised in homes where they are not taught about the importance of not being cruel to others.

CHAPTER 13

CONTROL YOUR DAUGHTERS ELECTRONIC USE

Electronics Are Bad Influences

Allowing your daughters to spend an enormous amount of time indoors will cripple their minds. Since computers and electronic use have taken over the world, a lot of girls are spending too much time indoors at the mall, watching television and videos, playing on the computer, and being on social media. It is important for your daughters to get exercise outdoors as well. They need at least twenty to thirty minutes of exercise a day. Exercising is good for your daughters' cardiovascular system and to develop their brains.

There is entirely too much nudity on television and videos and too much profanity in songs that are on the radio or on videos or on television. Parents should monitor what their daughters are watching and listening to on the radio. If parents do not do this, then you will see your daughters imitating what they see and hear on the television and on the radio. Some of the behavior that your daughters will see and hear is not appropriate for them and may have a negative influence on them. Most of the time the women that are in the videos on television or on the computer are not appropriately dressed and are not portraying themselves as self-confident women. These videos that your daughters may see and hear can have a bad influence on their mind.

It is okay for your daughters to love talking on their cell phones or being on social media if they do not let the cell phones control their every waking moment and thoughts. I suggest that parents have a time limit for allowing their daughters to be on social media and on a cell phone. I know how much fun being on social media is, but social media and electronic use can also be very addictive. This may interfere with your daughter's ability to get their school work completed and may affect their grades. Especially during the week when your daughters need to fully concentrate on their school work. No good can come from being addicted to social media or electronics. Consider having rules in your house about social media. On weekdays (Monday through Thursday), your daughters should have a time limit for using their electronics and being on social media. She cannot get on social media or use her cell phone until she is finished with her homework. Once she is finished with her homework, she is only allowed to be on social media or her cell phone for an hour or so. On weekends (Friday, Saturday, and Sunday), she can be on social media and use her cell phone for a longer time. If you notice a drop in any of her grades, then she should know that she can no longer be on social media or on her cell phone on the weekdays or the weekends until her grades improve.

Cell Phones Tempt Your Daughters To Text Late At Night

Seriously consider having your daughters, especially when they are teenagers, to turn their cell phones off at night and to give them to you at a certain time. The times may vary each day depending on whether it is a school night or the weekend. You may want to allow them to talk and text more on the weekends or holidays. Taking away their cell phones at night will allow them to not be tempted to text or talk on their cell phones throughout the night. Cell phones can be very distracting to your daughters and they may interfere with the amount of time that they rest at night. Your daughters need to get a certain amount of rest each night to do well in school the next day.

CHAPTER 14

HELP YOUR DAUGHTERS ACHIEVE ACADEMIC EXCELLENCE

Instill A Love Of Learning

Try to make learning fun and engaging so that your daughters will want to learn at school. Consider visiting local science centers, museums, and other educational places as well.

Parents should encourage their daughters to want to learn about various subject areas when they are very young. Your daughters will always feed off the energy of their parents. If you display excitement about learning different subject areas that your daughters are learning in school, then they will be excited to learn about them too. If parents show boredom, then your daughters will be bored as well and will not show enthusiasm to learn anything new.

Build Leadership Skills

Certain leadership skills are innate but other traits can be learned by your daughters. You should put your daughters in environments where they can learn to lead. One of the greatest characteristics of being a great leader is being able to inspire others to be their greatest and to dream big. Raise your daughters in a way so that they can be an inspiration to other girls.

Connect With Your Daughters' Teachers

Volunteer to be a chaperone and attend as many activities as possible with your daughters. This allows your daughters to learn about the world and cultural surroundings. Families that are involved in their children's education usually results in students that do better in school. It is important that parents evaluate their daughter's school every year to ensure that they are receiving a quality education. Observe your daughters' teachers, classmates, and surroundings, and you can learn what needs to be supplemented or what needs to be reinforced at your home. Stay in close contact with your daughter's teachers throughout the year to monitor their progress in school. Periodically email and schedule parent-teacher conferences with your daughter's teachers to find out the progress that your daughters are making in each of their subject areas. It is very important that parents have a good relationship with your daughters' teachers. At no time should you be trying to tell them how to teach in their classrooms, but you should always work with their teachers so that your daughters can continue to do better in school. Whenever your daughters are having trouble in a subject area then you should ask their teachers to suggest books, readings, or internet sites so that you can help your daughters understand the information. If this does not help, then you should consider hiring a tutor for your daughters.

Contacting a teacher to try and help your daughters improve her grades should not ever be a problem. Even if it is a problem, it is important to prepare your daughters for the next level of school. This is not just for now but also for later in your daughter's life. One reason that it should not be a problem will be your approach to the situation. Work directly with the teacher and figure out whether your daughters need to change her approach or study strategy at home or improve a study skill. The relationship between a teacher and parents should be a partnership.

Any prospective schools that your daughters may attend should be carefully considered. If money allows you to enroll your daughters in private or religious schools, that is great. These schools will keep their minds focused more than public schools and they will learn certain disciplines and practices that they will not learn if they are enrolled in public schools. Private school students are assigned homework that is more challenging to complete than public school students. Private school curriculums are more challenging and will better prepare your daughters academically for college than public school curriculums.

Attend High School Open Houses

It is a great idea to attend high school open houses two to three years before your daughters enter the ninth grade. This will give her the opportunity to meet potential teachers and other staff at a prospective high school. Ask questions about their teaching styles and about their curriculum. Take your daughters along to the open houses so that they can tour the school and ask any questions that they want as well. Another way to expose your daughters to a potential high school is by enrolling them in summer camps and other programs that are held for youth at the school. This is one of the ways that your daughters can meet different teachers and coaches at the high school she will attend. It is never too early to start exposing your daughters to the next level of school. I suggest that your daughters start going to potential high schools' open houses when she is in the sixth grade. She will thoroughly enjoy the visits and ask a lot of questions. Hopefully, she will ask good questions to the teachers and coaches that you might not have asked yourself. It truly will be a positive experience for your daughters.

Tour Colleges And Universities With Your Daughters

Visit as many colleges and universities as you can with your daughters. Expose your daughters to several colleges and universities from the time that she is young. These are priceless experiences where she will have the chance to meet and talk with college students about various issues.

Motivate Your Daughters Academically

Not enough girls are being encouraged and motivated by their parents to achieve academic excellence. Whenever I interact with a lot of parents, I notice that they are babying their daughters and making things as easy as possible for them and not pushing and motivating them to achieve academic excellence.

So many of these parents allow their daughters to constantly complain to them, even about the tiniest things. Whatever happened to letting girls know that they must work hard academically and in life to achieve whatever dreams and goals they have set for themselves and have them reinforce this with their actions? Whenever your daughters start complaining about something, you need to sternly remind them about working hard in school and in life as often as possible. This is a must so that they know that everything in their life, including academics, will not go their way or as they plan. Your daughters must be able to deal with disappointment, like low grades, and be able to rebound from it. The earlier that they learn this, the better able they will be to deal with these and other issues as well.

Your daughters will achieve academic excellence if they establish a daily study routine. If you start a study routine when your daughters are young they will always know what time to do their homework. Being able to focus should naturally become a part of your daughter's study routine because it will be a learned behavior for them. She should continue to follow a study routine and stay focused when completing her school work. Her routine may be that whenever she gets home from school she takes a short break to get a snack and relax for about thirty minutes and then immediately starts her homework. Hopefully, as your daughters become older she will get to the point where she will become more and more aware of when it is time for her to complete her homework, shower, eat her dinner, and go to bed.

Always prepare your daughters for the next level of school or the next grade. When she is a toddler, start preparing her for kindergarten. When she is in the fourth grade, start preparing her for middle school. When she is in middle school, start preparing her for high school. Work with your daughters to become more and more responsible and independent and how to keep herself as organized as possible with her school work. Establish a routine with her early, so she is always able to maintain good grades. Now keep in mind that when your daughters are transitioning from elementary school to middle school, or middle school to high school, you will need to allow an adjustment period for them. It may be a few weeks, or it may be an entire quarter or semester for them to adjust to their new school routine. Either way, try and be as patient as possible with your daughters. Your daughters will probably need a few weeks to adjust. When your daughters start kindergarten, begin reaching out well before Progress Report time to a teacher. Never wait until Progress Report time if you notice any low grades. In your daughter's case, determine what is a low grade for her. Watch her grades and whenever they are lower than that, get in touch with the teacher to find out how she can improve her grades.

Academic Extracurricular Activities Are Essential

Take as much time as possible to have your daughters participate in academic extracurricular activities. It will give your daughters a chance to learn outside the classroom in a fun environment. It is widely known that academic extracurricular activities can be a positive influence on your daughters.[3,4] Search around your local area for activities that may interest your daughters. Your local YMCA, county recreation centers, and local colleges and universities probably have something of interest to you and your daughters. A few suggestions are Science, Technology, Engineering, and Math (STEM) and Science, Technology, Engineering, Art, and Math (STEAM) Programs, Art Clubs, Math Clubs, Science Clubs, Language Clubs, Writing Clubs, and many other programs like these. The clubs can reinforce the subject material that your daughters are currently learning, recently learned, or learning in the future. It would be ideal if the program is sponsored by a local college or university. This will allow your daughters to be exposed to a college atmosphere at an early age.

Chapter 15

Establish Athletic Goals With Your Daughters

Involve Your Daughters In Sports

Sometimes, parents do not want their daughters to participate in sports. There is an impression that they will get hurt playing sports. Allow your daughters to participate in sports if they have the interest. If your daughters get involved in sports and then later decide that they do not want to participate anymore then remove them from the activity. Participating in sports builds teamwork, independence, self-confidence, the desire not to give up, and the desire to be successful. It will also allow your daughters to work well together with other girls, set priorities, and celebrate team accomplishments. If you enroll your daughter's in sports, then do not just drop them off for practices. Stay and talk with the coach after practices, watch your daughters' practices and give them additional one-on-one pointers, especially if you are a former athlete.

If you want your daughters to grow up to be mentally strong young women, then allow them to participate in sports. If your daughters participate in sports it will teach them that when they experience tough times to pick themselves up and keep going. Most of the time, mothers play a key role in whether their daughters participate in sports. If mothers do not want their daughters to participate in sports, then they usually do not. Individual training and coaching for your daughters may be good for them. It may be good for them to be a part of a sports team, but sometimes individual attention may be better for them. It will give your daughters a chance to ask questions and get individual attention. Consider coaching one of your daughters' sports teams. It will give you a chance to not only spend quality time with your daughters but for them to get hands-on teaching from you.

Do Not Over-Pressure Your Daughters To Get Athletic Scholarships

I talk to parents all the time who are consumed with pushing their young daughters too hard for them to get athletic scholarships to college. It is one thing to push and motivate your daughters to do their best. It is another thing to push your daughters into trying to get athletic college scholarships at an early age. Especially if you are trying to live through your daughters and have them accomplish something in their lives that you did not. Your daughters excelling in academics must be just as important to you as them excelling in sports. I talk with a lot of parents whose daughters are good in sports but do not have good grades. These girls may have a challenging time getting a high SAT score so that they can get into an exceptional college. What a total shame this is when it happens. Most of the time I blame the parents for not stressing the importance of education enough to their daughters at an early age. If parents did, then more girls would know the importance of education.

Parents should not bank on their daughters getting an athletic scholarship to college. They should not be over-bearing toward their daughters about it, either. Parents should have their daughters participate in sports for the right reasons. Let your daughters dream and make a path on their own and learn to also consider academic scholarships as well. Give your daughters a chance to dream and follow their own path in life.

So many parents enroll their young daughters in a sports program or team and never meet the coach or attend any of their games. Your daughters always need your support. You should want to know the adults that are spending time around your daughters and what they are teaching them and how they are possibly influencing their thinking. Parents should want to know what type of person the coach is. Is the coach building your daughter's self-confidence up or tearing it apart? The only way that parents will know this is by getting to know the coach. This cannot happen if parents never meet the coach or spend time with them. I have talked with numerous coaches that are amazed at the number of parents that only drop-off and pick-up their daughters from practice and that is the most interaction that they have with them. No parental involvement from them at all. Make sure that you are always supportive of your daughters even if you did not grow up participating in sports. It is still very important for you to watch your daughters' practices and games. A good youth coach will welcome parental involvement and support. Your parental involvement is another way to show that you care about your daughters and whom they are around. This is especially important if your daughters are young and impressionable.

I have interacted and noticed several things about a lot of competitive parents. A lot of their daughters are afraid to face their parents after they have not done well in a sport. Sometimes they delay having to go home so that they do not have to immediately see their parents. In some cases, their parents are mad when they have not done well. Some parents are just acting silly when they display negative energy like this toward their daughters. Some of these parents are former athletes themselves and were good and have the same expectations for their daughters. Some parents were not good in sports, so they put an enormous amount of pressure on their daughters because they want them to be good. Are these parents displaying negative behavior like this because they want their daughters to get an athletic scholarship to college? Whatever the reasons are, I hope that these parents will one day realize that they are damaging their daughters' self-confidence every time they display negative behavior like this toward them. These competitive parents may end up permanently damaging their daughters' self-esteem and self-confidence. Hopefully they can start catching themselves before they get so angry in these situations. Parents need to realize that it is not that serious. Let your daughters be themselves and stop putting so much pressure on them. Being good in sports should not be more important to parents than their daughters growing up with self-confidence. I never enjoy interacting with parents that act like this. Every time I interact with a parent that displays negative behavior like this I try to point out to them that not every girl is going to excel in sports. If your daughters do not excel in sports, then accept this and expose your daughters to as many other activities as you can to determine which ones they are good at. It may be that your daughters can participate in sports to build a healthy lifestyle that they can carry with them into adulthood. You as parents should want your daughters to do well, but not at their own expense. Realize that your daughter is her own individual and it is more important to show support toward her regardless of how well she does, not only in sports but with all other activities in her life as well.

Overbearing Sports Parents

If your daughters are involved in sports, it is important that parents talk with the coach whenever their daughters are not being motivated or uplifted, not just to complain. If you feel that your daughters are not doing well and could improve then there is no need to talk with the coach. Do not approach the coach with your daughters based on your daughters thinking that they are doing better than they did. This type of behavior sends a bad message to your daughters. It shows your daughters that you are willing to approach a coach even when your daughters are not doing well athletically instead of talking with them about the importance of working harder to improve. Your daughters are not always going to win in life, so they need to accept losing. I have talked with so many overbearing parents it was unreal. I am amazed at how so many parents are so driven for their daughters to do well in sports. Are these parents just as passionate about their daughters doing well in school? I doubt it, because most of the time I never hear these parents talk about how well their daughters are doing in school. They mostly talk about how good their daughters are in sports.

Parents sacrifice a lot of their personal time if their daughters participate in sports. They commit to taking their daughters back and forth to practices as well as to games. Sometimes the games are held locally but they can also be held regionally, especially if your daughters are on traveling sports teams. Some of the most demanding sports are track and swimming. Track and swim meets can last from early in the morning until very late in the afternoon and evening. So, if your daughters participate in track or swimming it will require a lot more of your time than some of the other sports.

CHAPTER 16

LOOK AHEAD IN YOUR DAUGHTER'S LIFE

Teach your daughters to always look ahead in life by setting goals for themselves. If goals are not set for your daughters, how will they know where they are trying to go in life? Consider buying toys, books, and other educational items that are a year or two, sometimes even three years older than your daughter is at the time. Also, buy age-appropriate toys for her in addition to the challenging items. From an early age teach your daughter to look ahead in life. When she is in elementary school start thinking about where she will go to middle school. When she is in middle school start thinking about where she will go to high school. When she is in high school think about where she will go to college. When your daughter is in college, she will need to think about what she will do to get started with a job and how she will make it happen.

Notes

1 Breastfeeding and Breast Milk: Condition Information, US National Institutes of Health.

2 W.L. Stuhldreher, Ph.D., Breastfeeding, Salem Press Encyclopedia of Science, January 2017.

3 A. Holland, and T. Andre, Participation in extracurricular activities in secondary school: what is known, what needs to be known?, Review of Educational Research, 57, 437-466, 1987.

4 M.J. Harvancik and G. Golsan, Academic success and participation in high school and extracurricular activities: Is there a relationship?, American Psychological Association Meeting, Washington, D.C., August 1986.